SEASONS

Fall

by Ann Herriges

BLASTOFF! READERS 3

BELLWETHER MEDIA • MINNEAPOLIS, MN

Note to Librarians, Teachers, and Parents:

Blastoff! Readers are carefully developed by literacy experts and combine standards-based content with developmentally appropriate text.

Level 1 provides the most support through repetition of high-frequency words, light text, predictable sentence patterns, and strong visual support.

Level 2 offers early readers a bit more challenge through varied simple sentences, increased text load, and less repetition of high-frequency words.

Level 3 advances early-fluent readers toward fluency through increased text and concept load, less reliance on visuals, longer sentences, and more literary language.

Whichever book is right for your reader, Blastoff! Readers are the perfect books to build confidence and encourage a love of reading that will last a lifetime!

This edition first published in 2007 by Bellwether Media.

No part of this publication may be reproduced in whole or in part without written permission of the publisher. For information regarding permission, write to Bellwether Media Inc., Attention: Permissions Department, Post Office Box 1C, Minnetonka, MN 55345-9998.

Library of Congress Cataloging-in-Publication Data
Herriges, Ann.
  Fall / by Ann Herriges.
    p. cm. — (Seasons) (Blastoff! readers)
Summary: "Simple text and supportive images introduce beginning readers to the characteristics of the season of fall. Intended for students in kindergarten through third grade."
  Includes bibliographical references and index.
  ISBN-10: 1-60014-033-5 (hardcover : alk. paper)
  ISBN-13: 978-1-60014-033-4 (hardcover : alk. paper)
  1. Autumn—Juvenile literature. I. Title. II. Series.
QB637.7.H47 2007
508.2—dc22   2006000614

Table of Contents

Fall comes after summer. Fall is a **season** of change.

The sun goes down earlier every day.

The air turns cool and crisp.

Frost covers the ground on cold mornings.

Ponds and lakes begin to **freeze**.

The wind
blows harder.

Wind blows
through dry plants
and scatters seeds.

Leaves turn red, yellow, orange, and brown.

The leaves fall to the ground. Soon the tree branches will be bare.

Animals get ready for winter.
Squirrels gather nuts and hide
them away.

Insects hide under logs and leaves. Earthworms crawl deep underground where the soil will not freeze.

Bears eat more. They look for a place to sleep through the winter.

Geese fly south to warmer places.

People get ready
for winter too.
They get out their
warm clothes.

Farmers **harvest crops**.

Gardeners plant **bulbs**. They will sprout into spring flowers.

Fall is the time for picking apples, playing football, and carving pumpkins.

Fall days grow colder and colder. You might even see snowflakes. That means winter is on the way.

Glossary

bulb—an onion-shaped part of a plant from which some flowers grow; tulips, daffodils, and irises are spring flowers that grow from bulbs.

crop—a plant that farmers grow in large amounts; wheat, corn, and potatoes are all crops.

freeze—to become solid; water turns to ice when the temperature is 32 degrees Fahrenheit (0 degrees Celsius).

frost—ice crystals that form on objects in freezing weather

harvest—to gather crops that are ripe

season—one of the four parts of the year; the seasons are spring, summer, fall, and winter.

To Learn More

AT THE LIBRARY
Florian, Douglas. *Autumnblings*. New York:
Greenwillow Books, 2003.

Glaser, Linda. *It's Fall*. Brookfield, Conn.: Millbrook
Press, 2001.

Lenski, Lois. *Now It's Fall*. New York: Random House, 2000.

Rockwell, Anne. *Four Seasons Make a Year*.
New York: Walker, 2004.

Rylant, Cynthia. *In November*. San Diego, Calif.:
Harcourt Brace, 2000.

Spinelli, Eileen. *I Know It's Autumn*. New York:
HarperCollins, 2004.

ON THE WEB
Learning more about the
seasons is as easy as 1, 2, 3.

1. Go to www.factsurfer.com

2. Enter "seasons" into search box.

3. Click the "Surf" button and you will see a list of
   related web sites.

With factsurfer.com, finding more information is just a
click away.

Index

The photographs in this book are reproduced through the courtesy of: VEER John Churchman/Getty Images, front cover; William Walsh, p. 4; Guy Bumgarner/Getty Images, p. 5; Chris Windsor/Getty Images, p. 6; Regina Chayer, p. 7; Willard Clay/Getty Images, pp. 8-9; Premium Stock/Getty Images, p. 9; William Radcliffe/Getty Images, p. 10; Art Wolfe/Getty Images, pp. 10-11; Michael Melford/Getty Images, p. 12; Val Corbett/ Getty Images, p. 13; Kristen Eckstien, p. 14; Raymond Gehman/Getty Images, p. 15; Andy Rouse/Getty Images, pp. 16-17; Seymour Hewitt/Getty Images, p. 17; Harald Sund/Getty Images, p. 18; Debrah McClinton/Getty Images, p. 19; Lori Adamski Peek/Getty Images, p. 20; Sandra O'Claire, p. 21.